Behind Closed Doors

What Lies Within

by Julius Williams III

Author Email: juliusw3.poetry@gmail.com

ISBN: 979-8-9934585-0-2

Dedication

To those who face internal battles…

I hope this book will help soothe your mind and heart, allowing you to untangle the knots of confusion that you might face.

You are not alone. Yet, there's undeniable beauty within the pain.

Enjoy, much love!

Before You Begin…

- *What parts of yourself have you silenced in order to survive?*

- *If someone opened the door to your inner world, what would they find that even you haven't faced yet?*

- *What does healing look like for you? Is it quiet? Messy? On-going?*

- *What's something you feel deeply but have never been able to fully explain out loud?*

- *Have you ever mistaken a breakdown for weakness—only to realize it was actually the beginning of clarity?*

Table of Content

Reflection & Identity

Love & Relationships

Illusions & Struggles

Lessons & Growth

Reflection & Identity

A Way with Words

'Been told I have a way with words,
Similar to the way the wind sings gracefully with the birds,
Or like the flow of a waterfall splashing against the rocks,
Much rather the fluttery heartbeat of a boy when his crush's eyes faithfully interlock.
Yet, its more related to the bigger things,
Maybe like the thoughts of our childhood's biggest dreams,
But less is more... at least as it seems,
Like subtle gestures is what I mean,
Instead of always wanting more, you must pause. Sit. Breathe.
Soak up the blessings of even the most minute, or in other words, little things.
The things we tend to forget to cherish,
But when it's gone, we cry, discombobulated, pondering, questioning like "where is it?"
Wow, maybe that's why they say I can have a way with words.
Yet, when I'm tired and feel unheard, I'm like *"away with words!"*
These senseless, audible messages just sound absurd,
Upset so my words may be slurred joined by teary eyes so my vision's blurred—

But maybe I'm overreacting, the reason may be due to an overflow of passion,
Hmm reminds me of the line about a waterfall, you see? It all correlates, so when you're alone, just sit for a moment and reflect on the choices you choose to make.
And if you wish to change in any way… know it isn't too late,
Just make sure you can uncomfortably manage the food you choose to put on your plate.
They say I have a way with words but most of these words will lie in my notes or in my head with no hope to escape,
Talk about a twisted fate…

Conversation

Let's sit down and have a conversation about how we feel...
Let's sit down and have a conversation about what's real...
To us, to our souls, to our inner deepest meaning...
The things we don't reveal...
The things that we hold close to our chest because for some odd reason we can't decide if this is how we should feel...
The things we choose to hide in our treasure chest until we can finally heal...
The things that inadvertently gets to us but we try to conceal...
The things! The things...
The things that pry at us and we wish they wouldn't...
The things that died and now brings us pain, in which we tried to rekindle yet the flame couldn't...
The things that we bare shackled to our shoulders, weighing heavy such as boulders, the regrets that we wish to hide behind our backs when facing our Beholder, though we shouldn't...
Or more so, are you willing to sit down and have a conversation?
A normal conversation... we can sit and talk about life and how blessed we are to be able to see, to hear, to live a life this free—

Because to me... even our struggles are a blessing, a bittersweet trial to see if even through pain, we can be joyous and maintain a positive perspective.
Because to me... even scars are beautiful.
Anything lacking authentic essence isn't suitable, because to be perfectly imperfectious is to be unique and this is something I choose to deem irrefutable.

So, I humbly ask you, will you bless me with a conversation?
We can sit or stand, you talk and I'll listen...
It can be humorous or about the things that make you worry and I'll wipe your eyes as they glisten,
There's more to you that I know I'm missing.
Are you ready to talk, because I'm ready to listen.

Empty Satisfaction

Endlessly traversing through the misty fog,
Spiraling across the sedated mountains of life,
Stumbling amongst the treacherous, vitality between the
quests set upon the mind, yet yielded from our own doing.
Or rather, leaping through the yelping joys of the floral fields,
Diving in the depths of the unprecedented waves of the
youthful fountain, more-or-less,
Squandering the vile 'ceptions of our very own shadows,
Obtaining the treasures sought out long before the rocky path
of rubble,
At last scrambling beneath the forgotten oasis... beneath the
dramatized spectacle of success and beauty... beneath the
supposedly meaningful tranquilities of life.
Yet, astonished to the realization of the falsified tales of the
anticipated treasure.
Void of the extravagant feeling of joy,
Ultimately left with some degree of blissful contentment, or
believed to be...
Truly left with the peculiar feeling of empty satisfaction.

The Daunting Question

As I lay down once again cradled in my nightly thoughts, a condemning question remains pinned to my mind.

A question unable to be waivered by thoughtless answers.

A question that isn't resolved by short and inadequate remarks.

A question so daunting to my heart... thriving to be sufficed, yet I'm unable to find sincerity within my response.

Therefore, I lay stunned in question of the choices I make.

Angel

As I struggled through the shattering crisp breeze of a lost and misconstrued oasis, tarnished with my anguished and crippled heart.
I found myself being uplifted by a dazzling angel.

Scars inches thick painted the angel in a unique manner.

As I wiped the dried tears of life from my clouded sight, I began to develop a sense of interest in what appeared to be an angelic figure… pure to the bone yet undeniably stamped with misfortunes, weighing it down as if chained to the mantle of the world.

If Only

Typically, I stray at night, paralyzed.

Frozen solid in my thoughts as if I am merely a painting on the wall.

Hung up on the confining chamber as an abstract display of art.
Stunned, running an uncountable number of lifetimes in my mind.

Searching for the perfect essence of life, the path of peace, the road towards serenity.

Somehow

Somehow, I'm the strongest person I know
But I'm also the weakest.
Somehow, I have the sight of an eagle

But the peripheral of a clam.
Somehow, I'm the happiest kid

But the saddest child.
Somehow, I'm free, yet enslaved to my past.
Somehow... I know I've found myself, but at times, I feel lost at sea as if I'm merely a speckle of sand.
Somehow, I feel immensely important yet tragically insignificant.
Somehow, I feel safe and protected yet I feel as if I'm bare, stuck in the middle of my monstrous thoughts, applaud... yet scorned, praised... yet shamed, loved... yet despised.
Somehow, I have the confidence of the most victorious champion, yet timid as an outcasted pup.
Somehow... I have the wisdom of an elderly man who've borne witness to all cycles of life, yet the functions of a new born.
Somehow, I have the might to take an army, but the strength of a slug on a walkway of salt—

Somehow… I'm covered in vicious scars, deep to the bone, yet healed by a phoenix, seemingly untouched by the wickedness of the world.

Somehow, I'm the biggest contradiction.

Somehow Extended

Somehow, I'm the strongest person I know
But I'm also the weakest.
Somehow, I have the sight of an eagle

But the peripheral of a clam.
Somehow, I'm the happiest kid

But the saddest child.
Somehow, I'm free, yet enslaved to my past.
Somehow… I know I've found myself, but at times, I feel lost at sea as if I'm merely a speckle of sand.
Somehow, I feel immensely important yet tragically insignificant.
Somehow, I feel safe and protected yet I feel as if I'm bare, stuck in the middle of my monstrous thoughts, applaud... yet scorned, praised... yet shamed, loved... yet despised.
Somehow, I have the confidence of the most victorious champion, yet timid as an outcasted pup.
Somehow… I have the wisdom of an elderly man who've borne witness to all cycles of life, yet the functions of a new born.
Somehow, I have the might to take an army, but the strength of a slug on a walkway of salt—

Somehow… I'm covered in vicious scars, deep to the bone, yet healed by a phoenix, seemingly untouched by the wickedness of the world.

Somehow, I'm the biggest contradiction.

Somehow, that's not all!

Somehow, you feel it! You've felt it! You understand it! You get it! Unable to shape it into words but...

Somehow, you can see it.

Somehow, tucked into the bottom of the draw, the back of the closet, hidden deep within the attic... put away but not forgotten.

Somehow, it's easier to relate to things we don't share.

Somehow, most things that are understood are rarely said.

Somehow, we are not shaped or molded by the success in our lives but the pain and bitter memories stored inside our hearts.

Somehow, we know pain, we know the setbacks, we are jointed at the hip of struggle yet we allow ourselves to pass it on to others.

Somehow, the words pouring out of our mouth contradict our very own actions.

Somehow, we seek answers and resolve for our daunting—

questions but sit inside afraid of what we'll find.
Somehow, these repetitive thoughts, these senseless emotions are constantly intertwined, causing so much friction—
between our minds and our hearts.
Somehow, yearning to be swaddled, held, kept at the warm breasts of comfort yet unwilling to let go of the burdens we carry.
Somehow, we want and we want but continue to pretend as if we're unable to change.
Somehow, we are content with our predicaments, too scared of what might replace our troubles.
Somehow...

Love & Relationships

5•12•24

Burned a few bridges searching for a truer connection,
Pray I be a man full of genuine love that can be seen through my new reflection,
Went from a lost pup to a man guided by God's direction,
Guess there's no point in stressin',
Loyalty and patience constantly in question,
Second guessin', *"am I truly a man that's destined?"*
Not necessarily for greatness but the bittersweet moments old couples tend to sit n' cherish,
"Oh Lord I know you're the fairest so please tell me what the fare is?"
Prepared it's fee could be tenfold,
Don't care just would love to turn old reminiscing on Ole goals,
Thinkin' bout stories untold while next to my forever "thing"
Hardest thing for me to ever dream,
Pray God you're listening,
Just want to be able to see some eyes glistening when missing me,
Maybe one day I'll realize what's meant to be...

Just Because

Just because... I put up with the purely distain, the mere disbandment of affection,
Just because... I choose to accept the vile, condemning onslaught of verbal tension,
Just because... I allow the unenjoyable memories to come forth and unfold repetitively,
Just because... I lie thoughtless upon the apparel of vanity as it lies conceited on its elevated pedestal,
Just because... I accept the misfortune presented at the foot of the broken canvas, painted in the most undesirable manner,
Just because... I unconditionally love you and all your audacious imperfections,
Just because... I care about the faded beauty of a miracle brought down from heaven,
Just because...

Our Story

The days of pain, the days of beauty,
The golden memories I had before you knew me,
The seamless nights with the sweetest dreams,
Early mornings under the sunlight's beam,
Not many worries or at least as it seems,

But time fly by with fluttery precision,
Mainly by myself, not necessarily my desired decision,
Then we stumbled crossing paths...
an unforeseen collision,
we argued... stubborn... needing to be right,
That's when things went quiet and we left,
Weeks go by and I began to notice how you're such a beauty,
Late night talks... that's when I finally understood you truly,
Then we fell in love... really happy as can be,
Fragile that's my heart's middle name but you healed me...
No longer felt the pain,
Kiss and mended all your aching scars... drying your tears
gently in the rain,
From that moment on, I knew without you, life wouldn't be the
same.

Blissful Beauty

Not certain what to say,
So I'll speak from a deeper part of my heart...
When I glance into your eyes,
I see nothing short of a blissful surprise,
The way life left marks on such an innocent beauty, mixed with the elegantly gentle smile
Of one of God's angels truly is... an extraordinary sight,
Not to mention the courageous spirit, jointed with love, blended together with a pinch of heavenly might
Is enough to make any stop... just long enough to notice and admire its beauty,
Though not just anyone can sit beside its spark,
Yet, its candle can illuminate a person's heart devoured by any type of dark...
It did for mine.
Yes, I still have hollow patches that are left behind,
Yes, I can't control all my thoughts so I tend to get lost in my mind,
Yes, what I think and what I feel often confuse me when they intertwine... yet,
Thanks to your joyous care I no longer have to walk alone—

With a heart as frozen as a crystal stone or a mind as shattered as an aging bone,
For you are a blissful beauty, better yet, you're one of God's angels truly...
Not perfect but perfectly imperfectious,
Short of divine but nevertheless inimitable,
Scarred yet it's the source of your beauty...
From the most sincere part of my heart,
I'm grateful we've met and because of you I'm better than the man I was before you knew me.

That Christmas Day

Empty.

Going through the motion, quite typical too
Void of a beat but what could I do?
Though, I open the door to a blissful beauty,
Catching the eyes of pure innocence truly.
Biggest smile with the youngest face,
Overflowing joy that could illuminate the world and space.
Received a hug that was very much needed,
Little did anyone know, I was very depleted.
Sparked a match to brighten my eyes,
But what I didn't know, was that there, lied a surprise.
Twisted knots of excited confusion,
Pray this isn't a part of my daily delusions.
Water filled my eyes as I opened the box,
Extremely grateful for the thought so I would've been joyous
for even a pair of socks.
In my hands a gift obtained,
As a million thoughts ran in my brain.
Suddenly, with emotions flowing,
I headed to the car before tears started going.
"Thank you, thank youu... it means a lot"—

Reliving the moment, thinking about how much joy it brought.
As the day continued, it kept getting better it seemed,
As we all spoked in the car sharing our biggest loves and
dreams.
Later eating food, laughing, and playing games
Then capturing memories, that in my mind, I hope they'll
remain.
Feeling humbly welcomed from the moment I arrived,
Then offered to stay the night so I graciously obliged.
As sleep highjacked my eyes I noticed one final surprise,
That on my very own face was a genuine smile and something
that I haven't felt in while,
Happy... feeling other emotions too,
I guess.. this is what *love* and *compassion* can do...

If We Ever Speak Again

If we ever speak again... I'd smile, indulging the beauty in the sparkling eyes God has blessed you with.
If we ever speak again... I'd ask how you've been, how's life, and if you're okay.
If we ever speak again... I'd tell you I'm proud of you for accomplishing the things you'd tell me were too far out of reach as we'd lay next to each other late at night.
If we ever speak again... I'd unveil how I've felt, how I feel, and the troubles you put me through.
If we ever speak again... I'd finally tell you paragraphs I was never able to utter.
If we ever speak again... I'd enlighten you to the continuous struggle of being mistreated, misunderstood, unheard by a person you love dearly.
If we ever speak again... I'd tell you that I never felt hatred but only love for you.
If we ever speak again... I'd hug you and thank you for all the loving memories you've blessed me with.
If we ever speak again... I'd remind you that I will always be here if you need me, that your beautiful even when you cry—

and that I love your beautiful imperfections.

If we ever speak again...

Feeling

This feeling... A weird one indeed,

Something desirable but I must maintain caution so downheartedly I can't proceed.

Twisted thoughts of confusion between my wants and my needs.

But this feeling, flooding my mind, yearning for more.

Overflowing with such a longing passion of intimacy,

more-or-less the feeling of the angelic butterflies flying gracefully in the midst of my stomach.

Such a feeling to crave...

Yet, it's pulling the strings of my heart like a worn-out rubber band, moments away from popping like confetti, unsure of what it might bring.

But, for some reason, I can't help but stand near the flames...

I don't wish to get burned but I can't help but love its warming embrace.

One thing is for sure; this is a dangerous feeling...

One to take with caution before things get too real.

Illusions & Struggles

Facade

Glistened with admiration,
Fulfilled with the thought of wealth,
Uplifted with the joyful spirit of successful,
Sufficed with the greed of desire,
Akin to the fixture of society,
Interconnected within the web of humanity,
Yet nevertheless trapped within the abyss... the facade... the misconstrued contentment of "*life*"
Unable to indulge into the beauty of the world and the intrinsic flow of genuine emotion,
Caught in the current of a ruthless tycoon of empty satisfaction.

Just Tell Me

Just tell me...

If there by any chance or any means that just maybe... maybe if things could be different, would you run to it? Would you prefer to roll down the window, tossing the book you created down the highway in hopes for a different story?

Just tell me...

Perhaps your heart is weary, suffocating from heavy regrets or maybe it's just the curiosity of the unknown... the multitude of avenues you could've pursued. The thought of possibly having more... such a dangerous drug. Like a game of Russian roulette.

So again, just tell me...

Is where you are at enough? Are you satisfied or is there more that you seek? Is your heart full or is your tolerance getting weak? Are you somewhat happy or genuinely content? Merely settling or pleased for how far you went?

It's interesting...

The grass isn't always greener on the other side and yet, you can't use the exact same flavors expecting a different taste—

I guess that's why they say if you're truly going to jump, at least look before you leap.

Star

When I sit and watch the stars,

I wonder if I can shine as bright.

Staying confidently admirable even in my darkest of nights.

Just maybe, I could also be a tiny beacon of hope no matter how far I may be.

Could I possibly create the same joy with the bright people around me?

I just wonder if I can be able to draw lovers closer with the flicker of light that lies within me.

Perhaps I can be as minuscule yet significant as even the smallest beam of hope in the midst of the darkest sky.

So, I wonder... *could I too be a reflection of such a humble star?*

A Moment

Just a moment...

That's all that it takes,

Take a deep breath,

Relax before making a careless mistake,

Sit or stand, call a loved one or maybe a close friend,

Vent or vibe, go for a walk or just chill inside,

Options...

Plenty to take, so many joys to consider rather than hastily making a mistake,

So please just try and take time to think, relax, or enjoy a drink because a lot can be lost in—

just a moment...

Lessons & Growth

Lesson

A lesson to be taught and a lesson to be learned,

That what we desire and seek with all our heart is something we must earn,

Not by doing great work or a million other chores but by stepping outside even when there's a storm to endure,

It's easy to want and want, and even need but sometimes we forget how to be grateful and our prayers turn into greed,

Yet, we're quick to take and take but take a huge step back when it's time for us to let go— as our old toys get replaced for the blessings we beg for— as if our baskets aren't already full,

That's the issue... *we tend to forget everything comes with a cost.*

Mixture of Both

A single tear tumbles down my face,

Followed by a couple more,

Not certain if it's tears of pain or more reluctantly… tears of joy,

Perhaps it's fueled by past traumas and heart aching decisions,

Or maybe it's the overflowing emotion of relief… glad that I survived the dreadful storm which single handedly caused me so much strife,

You know, the devastating lessons that we sadly learn about life,

Yet I'm ultimately grateful to be saved by God's provision,

Marking a new chapter where strength can be established by an intentional thought or envision.

Maybe So

I may have significant flaws,

So what I have broken bits of myself lying in my room,

Perhaps the light in my heart does tend to flicker in the midst of the night,

Yes, I may be weak and tenderhearted,

But I am more than the very scars on my back,

I am greater than the shackles I am tied to,

I am stronger than the constraining burdens of my past,

I will continue to march down the beaten path even if my candlestick blows out,

Because... *I am more than what meets the eye.*

Poetry

To me, poetry is a means

To relate, to connect

To mirror, to reflect

To dream, to assess… the memories of our soul, of our flesh

To relive, or forget

To acknowledge our growth or regress

To unwind and limit our stress

To be free with the way that we dress

To make time to be a mess

To take hold of the freedom that we possess…

To me, that is the means of poetry.

Closed Door

Sitting behind *my closed door, my sanctuary, my freedom and safety*... I no longer have to face or put up with the painful troubles accompanied with life. I can let go, cry, laugh and let my imagination run wild with no regards to another's opinion or backlash.

Yet, sometimes I wonder how *a place of peace, a refuge* from worry and despair— or much rather *a home of security* can become a prison cell... trapped... confined... left to remain separated from the outside— ultimately avoiding looking in the mirror, to rather stay in a box of *shelter* where there's no need to unmask issues from within. To settle with my eyes closed because the glare of ownership, growth, and the unknown can be quite unbearable to face and remaining ignorant to it all is much easier.

I guess, similarly to a lot of things in life, there's a fine line between what's good and unhealthy. Seeking that balance is one of the joys of life, as it gives us something to strive for... *so maybe one day we can confidently open our closed door.*

About the Author

Julius Williams III is a writer, athlete, and dreamer born in Spartanburg, South Carolina. A graduate of the Class of 2024 at Wetumpka High and a student-athlete at the University of Alabama in Huntsville, since 2024. He is pursuing a professional athletic career while nurturing his love for words.

Through poetry, Julius channels the quiet struggles, deep reflections, and fragile hopes that often remain hidden *'behind closed doors.'* His work speaks to resilience, faith, and the unspoken battles that shape us all.

This debut collection is a testimony to survival, growth, and the beauty found in contradiction.

"Scars are remarkably beautiful. It signifies strength and empowerment as not only a survivor but a thriver."

www.ingramcontent.com/pod-product-compliance
Lightning Source LLC
LaVergne TN
LVHW090618110826
845146LV00001B/446

* 9 7 9 8 9 9 3 4 5 8 5 0 2 *